MW01294099

Principal Doctrines

Principal Doctrines

By

Epicurus

Enhanced Media
2016

Principal Doctrines of Epicurus. From Book X of *Lives and Opinions of Eminent Philosophers* by Diogenes Laërtius. Translated by Charles Duke Yonge, 1853.

The Epicurean Pursuit of Pleasure by William De Witt Hyde. First published in *The Five Great Philosophies of Life* by William De Witt Hyde in 1911.

Epicurus by Charles Bradlaugh. First published in *Ancient and Modern Celebrated Freethinkers*, 1877.

Published by Enhanced Media.

Enhanced Media Publishing
Los Angeles, CA.

First Printing: 2016.

ISBN-13: 978-1523790074

ISBN-10: 1523790075

Contents

1. That which is happy and imperishable, neither has trouble itself, nor does it cause it to anything; so that it is not subject to the feelings of either anger or gratitude; for these feelings only exist in what is weak.

2. Death is nothing to us; for that which is dissolved is devoid of sensation, and that which is devoid of sensation is nothing to us.

3. The limit of the greatness of the pleasures is the removal of everything which can give pain. And where pleasure is, as long as it lasts, that which gives pain, or that which feels pain, or both of them, are absent.

4. Pain does not abide continuously in the flesh, but in its extremity it is present only a very short time. That pain which only just exceeds the pleasure in the flesh, does not last many days. But long diseases have in them more that is pleasant than painful to the flesh.

5. It is not possible to live pleasantly without living prudently, and honourably, and justly; nor to live prudently, and honourably, and justly, without living pleasantly. But he to whom it does not happen to live prudently, honourably, and justly, cannot possibly live pleasantly.

6. For the sake of feeling confidence and security with regard to men, and not with reference to the nature of government and kingly power being a good, some men have wished to be eminent and powerful, in order that others might attain this feeling by their means; thinking that so they would secure safety as far as men are concerned. So that, if the life of such men is safe, they have attained to the nature of good; but if it is not safe, then they have failed in obtaining that for the sake of which they originally desired power according to the order of nature.

7. No pleasure is intrinsically bad: but the efficient causes of some pleasures bring with them a great many perturbations of pleasure.

8. If every pleasure were condensed, if one may so say, and if each lasted long, and affected the whole body, or the essential parts of it, then there would be no difference between one pleasure and another.

9. If those things which make the pleasures of debauched men, put an end to the fears of the mind, and to those which arise about the heavenly bodies, and death, and pain; and if they taught us what ought to be the limit of our desires, we should have no pretence for blaming those who wholly devote themselves to pleasure, and who never feel any pain or grief (which is the chief evil) from any quarter.

10. If apprehensions relating to the heavenly bodies did not disturb us, and if the terrors of death have no concern with us, and if we had the courage to contemplate the boundaries of pain and of the desires, we should have no need of physiological studies.

11. It would not be possible for a person to banish all fear about those things which are called most essential, unless he knew what is the nature of the universe, or if he had any idea that the fables told about it could be true; and therefore, it is, that a person cannot enjoy unmixed pleasure without physiological knowledge.

12. It would be no good for a man to secure himself safety as far as men are concerned, while in a state of apprehension as to all the heavenly bodies, and those under the earth, and in short, all those in the infinite.

13. Irresistible power and great wealth may, up to a certain point, give us security as far as men are concerned; but the security of men in general depends upon the tranquillity of their souls, and their freedom from ambition.

14. The riches of nature are defined and easily procurable; but vain desires are insatiable.

15. The wise man is but little favoured by fortune; but his reason procures him the greatest and most valuable goods, and these he does enjoy, and will enjoy the whole of his life.

16. The just man is the freest of all men from disquietude; but the unjust man is a perpetual prey to it.

17. Pleasure in the flesh is not increased, when once the pain arising from want is removed; it is only diversified.

18. The most perfect happiness of the soul depends on these reflections, and on opinions of a similar character on all those questions which cause the greatest alarm to the mind.

19. Infinite and finite time both have equal pleasure, if any one measures its limits by reason.

20. If the flesh could experience boundless pleasure, it would want to dispose of eternity.

21. But reason, enabling us to conceive the end and dissolution of the body, and liberating us from the fears relative to eternity, procures for us all the happiness of which life is capable, so completely that we have no further occasion to include eternity in our desires. In this disposition of mind, man is happy even when his troubles engage him to quit life; and to die thus, is for him only to interrupt a life of happiness.

22. He who is acquainted with the limits of life knows, that that which removes the pain which arises from want, and which makes the whole of life perfect, is easily procurable; so that he has no need of those things which can only be attained with trouble.

23. But as to the subsisting end, we ought to consider it with all the clearness and evidence which we refer to whatever we think and believe; otherwise, all things will be full of confusion and uncertainty of judgment.

24. If you resist all the senses, you will not even have anything left to which you can refer, or by which you may be able to judge of the falsehood of the senses which you condemn.

25. If you simply discard one sense, and do not distinguish between the different elements of the judgment, so as to know on the one hand, the induction which goes beyond the actual sensation, or, on the other, the actual and immediate notion; the affections, and all the conceptions of the mind which lean directly on the sensible representation, you will be imputing trouble into the other sense, and destroying in that quarter every species of criterion.

26. If you allow equal authority to the ideas, which, being only inductive, require to be verified, and to those which bear about them an immediate certainty, you will not escape error; for you will be confounding

doubtful opinions with those which are not doubtful, and true judgments with those of a different character.

27. If, on every occasion, we do not refer every one of our actions to the chief end of nature, if we turn aside from that to seek or avoid some other object, there will be a want of agreement between our words and our actions.

28. Of all the things which wisdom provides for the happiness of the whole life, by far the most important is the acquisition of friendship.

29. The same opinion encourages man to trust that no evil will be everlasting, or even of long duration; as it sees that, in the space of life allotted to us, the protection of friendship is most sure and trustworthy.

30. Of the desires, some are natural and necessary, some natural, but not necessary, and some are neither natural nor necessary, but owe their existence to vain opinions.

31. Those desires which do not lead to pain, if they are not satisfied, are not necessary. It is easy to impose silence on them when they appear difficult to gratify, or likely to produce injury.

32. When the natural desires, the failing to satisfy which is, nevertheless, not painful, are violent and obstinate, it is a proof that there is an admixture of vain opinion in them; for then energy does not arise from their own nature, but from the vain opinions of men.

33. Natural justice is a covenant of what is suitable, leading men to avoid injuring one another, and being injured.

34. Those animals which are unable to enter into an argument of this nature, or to guard against doing or sustaining mutual injury, have no such thing as justice or injustice. And the case is the same with those nations, the members of which are either unwilling or unable to enter into a covenant to respect their mutual interests.

35. Justice has no independent existence; it results from mutual contracts, and establishes itself wherever there is a mutual engagement to guard against doing or sustaining mutual injury.

36. Injustice is not intrinsically bad; it has this character only because there is joined with it a fear of not escaping those who are appointed to punish actions marked with that character.

37. It is not possible for a man who secretly does anything in contravention of the agreement which men have made with one another, to guard against doing, or sustaining mutual injury, to believe that he shall always escape notice, even if he have escaped notice already ten thousand times; for, till his death, it is uncertain whether he will not be detected.

38. In a general point of view, justice is the same thing to every one; for there is something advantageous in mutual society. Nevertheless, the difference of place, and divers other circumstances, make justice vary.

39. From the moment that a thing declared just by the law is generally recognized as useful for the mutual relations of men, it becomes really just, whether it is universally regarded as such or not.

40. But if, on the contrary, a thing established by law is not really useful for the social relations, then it is not just; and if that which was just, inasmuch as it was useful, loses this character, after having been for some time considered so, it is not less true that, during that time, it was really just, at least for those who do not perplex themselves about vain words, but who prefer, in every case, examining and judging for themselves.

41. When, without any fresh circumstances arising, a thing which has been declared just in practice does not agree with the impressions of reason, that is a proof that the thing was not really just. In the same way, when in consequence of new circumstances, a thing which has been pronounced just does not any longer appear to agree with utility, the thing which was just, inasmuch as it was useful to the social relations and intercourse of mankind, ceases to be just the moment when it ceases to be useful.

42. He who desires to live tranquilly without having any thing to fear from other men, ought to make himself friends; those whom he cannot make friends of, he should, at least, avoid rendering enemies; and if that is not in his power, he should, as far as possible, avoid all intercourse with them, and keep them aloof, as far as it is for his interest to do so.

43. The happiest men are they who have arrived at the point of having nothing to fear from those who surround them. Such men live with one an-

other most agreeably, having the firmest grounds of confidence in one another, enjoying the advantages of friendship in all their fulness, and not lamenting, as a pitiable circumstance, the premature death of their friends.

Selections from the Epicurean scriptures

Epicureanism is so simple a philosophy of life that it scarcely needs interpretation. In fact, as the following citations show, it was originally little more than a set of directions for living "the simple life," with pleasure as the simplifying principle. The more subtle teaching of the other philosophies will require to be introduced by explanatory statement, or else accompanied by a running commentary as it proceeds. The best way to understand Epicureanism, however, is to let Epicurus and his disciples speak for themselves. Accordingly, as in religious services the sermon is preceded by reading of the Scriptures and singing of hymns, we will open our study of the Epicurean philosophy of life by selections from their scriptures and hymns. First the master, though unfortunately he is not so good a master of style as many of his disciples, shall speak. The gist of Epicurus's teaching is contained in the following passages.

"The end of all our actions is to be free from pain and fear; and when once we have attained this, all the tempest of the soul is laid, seeing that the living creature has not to go to find something that is wanting, or to seek something else by which the good of the soul and of the body will be fulfilled."

"Wherefore we call pleasure the alpha and omega of a blessed life. Pleasure is our first and kindred good. From it is the commencement of every choice and every aversion, and to it we come back, and make feeling the rule by which to judge of every good thing."

"When we say, then, that pleasure is the end and aim, we do not mean the pleasures of the prodigal, or the pleasures of sensuality, as we are understood by some who are either ignorant and prejudiced for other views, or inclined to misinterpret our statements. By pleasure we mean the absence of pain in the body and trouble in the soul. It is not an unbroken succession of drinking feasts and of revelry, not the enjoyments of the fish and other delicacies of a splendid table, which produce a pleasant life: it is sober reasoning, searching out the reasons for every choice and avoidance, and banishing those beliefs through which great tumults take possession of the soul."

"Nothing is so productive of cheerfulness as to abstain from meddling, and not to engage in difficult undertakings, nor force yourself to do something beyond your power. For all this involves your nature in tumults."

"The main part of happiness is the disposition which is under our own control. Service in the field is hard work, and others hold command. Public speaking abounds in heart-throbs and in anxiety whether you can carry conviction. Why then pursue an object like this, which is at the disposal of others?"

"Wealth beyond the requirements of nature is no more benefit to men than water to a vessel which is full. Both alike overflow. We can look upon another's goods without perturbation and can enjoy purer pleasure than they, for we are free from their arduous struggle."

"Thou must also keep in mind that of desires some are natural, and some are groundless; and that of the natural some are necessary as well as natural, and some are natural only. And of the necessary desires, some are necessary if we are to be happy, and some if the body is to remain unperturbed, and some if we are even to live. By the clear and certain understanding of these things we learn to make every preference and aversion, so that the body may have health and the soul tranquillity, seeing that this is the sum and end of a blessed life."

"Cheerful poverty is an honourable thing."

"Great wealth is but poverty when matched with the law of nature."

"If any one thinks his own not to be most ample, he may become lord of the whole world, and will yet be wretched."

"Fortune but slightly crosses the wise man's path."

"If thou wilt make a man happy, add not unto his riches, but take away from his desires."

"And since pleasure is our first and native good, for that reason we do not choose every pleasure whatsoever, but oftentimes pass over many pleasures when a greater annoyance ensues from them. And oftentimes we consider pains superior to pleasures, and submit to the pain for a long time, when it is attended for us with a greater pleasure. All pleasure, therefore, because of its kinship with our nature, is a good, but it is not in all cases our choice, even as every pain is an evil, though pain is not always, and in every case, to be shunned."

"It is, however, by measuring one against another, and by looking at the conveniences and inconveniences, that all these things must be judged. Sometimes we treat the good as an evil, and the evil, on the contrary, as a good; and we regard independence of outward goods as a great good, not so as in all cases to use little, but so as to be contented with little, if we have not much, being thoroughly persuaded that they have the sweetest enjoyment of luxury who stand least in need of it, and that whatever is natural is easily procured, and only the vain and worthless hard to win. Plain fare gives as much pleasure as a costly diet, when once the pain due to want is removed; and bread and water confer the highest pleasure when they are brought to hungry lips. To habituate self, therefore, to plain and inexpensive diet gives all that is needed for health, and enables a man to meet the necessary requirements of life without shrinking, and it places us in a better frame when we approach at intervals a costly fare, and renders us fearless of fortune."

"Riches according to nature are of limited extent, and can be easily procured; but the wealth craved after by vain fancies knows neither end nor limit. He who has understood the limits of life knows how easy it is to get all that takes away the pain of want, and all that is required to make our life perfect at every point. In this way he has no need of anything which involves a contest."

"The beginning and the greatest good is prudence. Wherefore prudence is a more precious thing even than philosophy: from it grow all the other virtues, for it teaches that we cannot lead a life of pleasure which is not also a life of prudence, honour, and justice; nor lead a life of prudence, honour, and justice, which is not also a life of pleasure. For the virtues have grown into one with a pleasant life, and a pleasant life is inseparable from them."

"Of all the things which wisdom procures for the happiness of life as a whole, by far the greatest is the acquisition of friendship."

"We ought to look round for people to eat and drink with, before we look for something to eat and drink: to feed without a friend is the life of a lion and a wolf."

"Do everything as if Epicurus had his eye upon you. Retire into yourself chiefly at that time when you are compelled to be in a crowd."

"We ought to select some good man and keep him ever before our eyes, so that we may, as it were, live under his eye, and do everything in his sight."

"No one loves another except for his own interest."

"Among the other ills which attend folly is this: it is always beginning to live."

"A foolish life is restless and disagreeable: it is wholly engrossed with the future."

"We are born once: twice we cannot be born, and for everlasting we must be non-existent. But thou, who art not master of the morrow, puttest off the right time. Procrastination is the ruin of life for all; and, therefore, each of us is hurried and unprepared at death."

"Learn betimes to die, or if it please thee better to pass over to the gods."

"He who is least in need of the morrow will meet the morrow most pleasantly."

"Injustice is not in itself a bad thing: but only in the fear, arising from anxiety on the part of the wrong-doer, that he will not escape punishment."

"A wise man will not enter political life unless something extraordinary should occur."

"The free man will take his free laugh over those who are fain to be reckoned in the list with Lycurgus and Solon."

"The first duty of salvation is to preserve our vigour and to guard against the defiling of our life in consequence of maddening desires."

"Accustom thyself in the belief that death is nothing to us, for good and evil are only where they are felt, and death is the absence of all feeling: therefore a right understanding that death is nothing to us makes enjoyable the mortality of life, not by adding to years an illimitable time, but by taking away the yearning after immortality. For in life there can be nothing to fear, to him who has thoroughly apprehended that there is nothing to cause fear in what time we are not alive. Foolish, therefore, is the man who says that he fears death, not because it will pain when it comes, but because it pains in the prospect. Whatsoever causes no annoyance when it is present causes only a groundless pain by the expectation thereof. Death, therefore, the most awful of evils, is nothing to us, seeing that when we are, death is not yet, and when death comes, then we are not. It is nothing then, either to the living or the dead, for it is not found with the living, and the dead exist no longer."

These words of the master, given with no attempt to reconcile their apparent inconsistencies, convey very fairly the substance of his teaching, including both its excellences and its deep defects. The exalted esteem in which his doctrines were held, leading his disciples to commit them to memory as sacred and verbally inspired; the personal reverence for his character; and the extravagant expectations as to what his philosophy was to do for the world, together with a glimpse into the Epicurean idea of heaven, are well illustrated by the following sentences at the opening of the third book of Lucretius, addressed to Epicurus:—

"Thee, who first wast able amid such thick darkness to raise on high so bright a beacon and shed a light on the true interests of life, thee I follow, glory of the Greek race, and plant now my footsteps firmly fixed in thy imprinted marks, not so much from a desire to rival thee as that from the love I bear thee I yearn to imitate thee. Thou, father, art discoverer of things, thou furnishest us with fatherly precepts, and like as bees sip of all things in the flowery lawns, we, O glorious being, in like manner, feed from out thy pages upon all the golden maxims, golden I say, most worthy ever of endless life. For soon as thy philosophy issuing from a godlike intellect has begun with loud voice to proclaim the nature of things, the terrors of the mind are dispelled, the walls of the world part asunder, I see things in operation throughout the whole void: the divinity of the gods is revealed, and their tranquil abodes which neither winds do shake, nor clouds drench with rains nor snow congealed by sharp frost harms with hoary fall: an ever cloudless ether o'ercanopies them, and they laugh with light shed largely round. Nature too supplies all their wants, and nothing ever impairs their peace of mind."

Horace is so saturated with Epicureanism that it is hard to select any one of his odes as more expressive of it than another. His ode on the "Philosophy of Life" perhaps presents it in as short compass as any. He asks what he shall pray for? Not crops, and ivory, and gold gained by laborious and risky enterprise; but healthy, solid contentment with the simple, universal pleasures near at hand.

"Why to Apollo's shrine repair
New hallowed? Why present with prayer
Libation? Not those crops to gain,
Which fill Sardinia's teeming plain,
"Herds from Calabria's sunny fields,
Nor ivory that India yields,
Nor gold, nor tracts where Liris glides
So noiseless down its drowsy sides.
"Blest owners of Calenian vines,
Crop them; ye merchants, drain the wines,
That cargoes brought from Syria buy,
In cups of gold. For ye, who try
"The broad Atlantic thrice a year
And never drown, must sure be dear
To gods in heaven. Me—small my need—
Light mallows, olives, chiccory, feed.
"Give me then health, Apollo; give
Sound mind; on gotten goods to live
Contented; and let song engage
An honoured, not a base, old age."

For a lesson from the new Epicurean testament we cannot do better than turn to the sensible pages of Herbert Spencer's *Data of Ethics*.

"The pursuit of individual happiness within those limits prescribed by social conditions is the first requisite to the attainment of the greatest general happiness. To see this it needs but to contrast one whose self-regard has maintained bodily well-being with one whose regardlessness of self has brought its natural results; and then to ask what must be the contrast between two societies formed of two such kinds of individuals.

"Bounding out of bed after an unbroken sleep, singing or whistling as he dresses, coming down with beaming face ready to laugh on the smallest provocation, the healthy man of high powers, conscious of past successes and, by his energy, quickness, resource, made confident of the future, enters on the day's business not with repugnance but with gladness; and from hour to hour experiencing satisfactions from work effectually done, comes home with an abundant surplus of energy remaining for hours of relaxation. Far otherwise is it with one who is enfeebled by great neglect of self. Already deficient, his energies are made more deficient by constant endeavours to execute tasks that prove beyond his strength, and by the resulting discouragement. Hours of leisure which, rightly passed, bring pleasures that raise the tide of life and renew the powers of work, cannot be utilized: there is not vigour enough for enjoyments involving action, and lack of spirits prevents passive enjoyments from being entered upon with zest. In brief, life becomes a burden. Now if, as must be admitted, in a community composed of individuals like the first the happiness will be relatively great, while in one composed of individuals like the last there will be relatively little happiness, or rather much misery; it must be admitted that conduct causing the one result is good and conduct causing the other is bad.

"He who carries self-regard far enough to keep himself in good health and high spirits, in the first place thereby becomes an immediate source of happiness to those around, and in the second place maintains the ability to increase their happiness by altruistic actions. But one whose bodily vigour and mental health are undermined by self-sacrifice carried too far, in the first place becomes to those around a cause of depression, and in the second place renders himself incapable, or less capable, of actively furthering their welfare.

"Full of vivacity, the one is ever welcome. For his wife he has smiles and jocose speeches; for his children stores of fun and play; for his friends pleasant talk interspersed with the sallies of wit that come from buoyancy. Contrariwise, the other is shunned. The irritability resulting now from ailments, now from failures caused by feebleness, his family has daily to bear. Lacking adequate energy for joining in them, he has at best but a tepid interest in the amusements of his children; and he is called a wet blanket by his friends. Little account as our ethical reasonings take note of it, yet is the fact obvious that since happiness and misery are infectious, such regard for self as conduces to health and high spirits is a benefaction to others, and such disregard of self as brings on suffering, bodily or mental, is a malefaction to others.

"The adequately egoistic individual retains those powers which make altruistic activities possible. The individual who is inadequately egoistic loses more or less of his ability to be altruistic. The truth of the one proposition is self-evident; and the truth of the other is daily forced on us by examples. Note a few of them. Here is a mother who, brought up in the insane fashion usual among the cultivated, has a physique not strong enough for suckling her infant, but who, knowing that its natural food is the best, and anxious for its welfare, continues to give milk for a longer time than her system will bear. Eventually the accumulating reaction tells. There comes exhaustion running, it may be, into illness caused by depletion; occasionally ending in death, and often entailing chronic weakness. She becomes, perhaps for a time, perhaps permanently, incapable of carrying on household affairs; her other children suffer from the loss of maternal attention; and where the income is small, payments for nurse and doctor tell injuriously on the whole family. Instance, again, what not unfrequently happens with the father. Similarly prompted by a high sense of obligation, and misled by current moral theories into the notion that self-denial may rightly be carried to any extent, he daily continues his office work for long hours regardless of hot head and cold feet; and debars himself from social pleasures, for which he thinks he can afford neither time nor money. What comes of this entirely unegoistic course? Eventually a sudden collapse, sleeplessness, inability to work. That rest which he would not give himself when his sensations prompted he has now to take in long measure. The extra earnings laid by for the benefit of his family are quickly swept away by costly journeys in aid of recovery and by the many expenses which illness entails. Instead of increased ability to do his duty by his offspring there comes now inability. Lifelong evils on them replace hoped-for goods. And so is it, too, with the social effects of inadequate egoism. All grades furnish examples of the mischiefs, positive and negative, inflicted on society by excessive neglect of self. Now the case is that of a labourer who, conscientiously continuing his work under a broiling sun, spite of violent protests from his feelings, dies of sunstroke; and leaves his family a burden to the parish. Now the case is that of a clerk whose eyes permanently fail from overstraining, or who, daily writing for hours after his fingers are painfully cramped, is attacked with 'scrivener's palsy,' and, unable to write at all, sinks with aged parents into poverty which friends are called on to mitigate.

"And now the case is that of a man devoted to public ends who, shattering his health by ceaseless application, fails to achieve all he might have achieved by a more reasonable apportionment of his time between labour on behalf of others, and ministration to his own needs."

After this lengthy prose extract, let us turn to the modern Epicurean poets.

At once the best and the worst rendering of Epicureanism into verse is Fitzgerald's translation of Omar Khayyam. It is the best because of the frankness with which it draws out to its logical conclusion, in a cynical despair of everything nobler than the pleasure of the moment, the consequences of identifying the self with mere pleasure-seeking. It is the worst because, instead of presenting Epicureanism mixed with nobler elements, as Walt Whitman and Stevenson do, it gives us the pure and undiluted article as a final gospel of life. The fact that it has proved such a fad during the past few years is striking evidence of the husky fare on which our modern prodigals can be content to feed.

"Come fill the Cup, and in the fire of Spring
Your Winter-garment of repentance fling:
The bird of Time has but a little way
To flutter—and the Bird is on the Wing.
"A Book of Verses underneath the Bough,
A Jug of Wine, a Loaf of Bread—and Thou
Beside me singing in the Wilderness—
Oh, Wilderness were Paradise enow.
"Ah, my Beloved, fill the Cup that clears
To-day of past Regrets and future Fears:
To-morrow!—Why, To-morrow I may be
Myself with Yesterday's Sev'n thousand Years.
"I sent my soul through the Invisible,
Some letter of that After-life to spell:
And by and by my Soul return'd to me,
And answer'd, "I myself am Heav'n and Hell:
"Heav'n but the vision of fulfill'd Desire,
And Hell the Shadow of a Soul on Fire,
Cast on the Darkness into which Ourselves,
So late emerged from, shall so soon expire."

From this melancholy attempt to offer us Epicureanism as a complete account of life, overshadowed as it is by the gloom of the Infinite which the man who stakes his all on momentary pleasure feels doomed to forego, it is a relief to turn to men who strike cheerfully and firmly the Epicurean note; but pass instantly on to blend it with sterner notes and larger views of life, in which it plays its essential, yet strictly subordinate part.

Of all the men who thus strike scattered Epicurean notes, without attempting the impossible task of making a harmonious and satisfactory tune out of them, our American Pagan, Walt Whitman, is the best example.

"What is commonest, cheapest, nearest, easiest, is Me,
Me going in for my chances, spending for vast returns,
Adorning myself to bestow myself on the first that will take me,
Not asking the sky to come down to my good will,
Scattering it freely forever.
"O the joy of manly self-hood!
To be servile to none, to defer to none,
not to any tyrant known or unknown,
To walk with erect carriage, a step springy and elastic,
To look with calm gaze or with flashing eye,
To speak with a full and sonorous voice out of a broad chest,
To confront with your personality all the other personalities
of the earth.
"O while I live to be the ruler of life, not a slave,
To meet life as a powerful conqueror,
No fumes, no ennui, no more complaints or scornful criticisms,
To these proud laws of the air, the water, and the ground,
proving my interior soul impregnable,
And nothing exterior shall ever take command of me.
"For not life's joys alone I sing, repeating—the joy of death!
The beautiful touch of death, soothing and benumbing a few moments,
for reasons,
Myself discharging my excrementitious body to be burn'd,
or render'd to powder, or buried,
My real body doubtless left to me for other spheres,
My voided body nothing more to me, returning to the purifications,
further offices, eternal uses of the earth.
"O to have life henceforth a poem of new joys!
To dance, clap hands, exult, shout, skip, leap, roll on, float on!
To be a sailor of the world bound for all ports,
A swift and swelling ship full of rich words, full of joys."

Whitman, with this wild ecstasy, to be sure is an Epicurean and something more. Indeed, pure Epicureanism, unmixed with better elements, is rather hard to find in modern literature. One other hymn, by Robert Louis Stevenson, likewise adds to pure Epicureanism a note of strenuous intensity in the great task of happiness which was foreign to the more easy-going form of the ancient doctrine. In Stevenson Epicureanism is only a flavour to more substantial viands.

The Celestial Surgeon

"If I have faltered more or less
In my great task of happiness;
If I have moved among my race
And shown no glorious morning face;
If beams from happy human eyes
Have moved me not; if morning skies,
Books, and my food, and summer rain
Knocked on my sullen heart in vain:—
Lord, thy most pointed pleasure take
And stab my spirit broad awake!
Or, Lord, if too obdurate I,
Choose thou, before that spirit die,
A piercing pain, a killing sin,
And to my dead heart run them in."

While we are with Stevenson, we may as well conclude our selections from the Epicurean scriptures in these words from his Christmas Sermon: "Gentleness and cheerfulness, these come before all morality: they are the perfect duties. If your morals make you dreary, depend upon it they are wrong. I do not say, 'give them up,' for they may be all you have; but conceal them like a vice, lest they should spoil the lives of better men."

The Epicurean view of work and play

Pleasure is our great task, "the gist of life, the end of ends." To be happy ourselves and radiating centres of happiness to choice circles of congenial friends,—this is the Epicurean ideal. The world is a vast reservoir of potential pleasures. Our problem is to scoop out for ourselves and our friends full measure of these pleasures as they go floating by. We did not make the world. It made itself by a fortuitous concourse of atoms. It would be foolish for us to try to alter it. Our only concern is to get out of it all the pleasure we can; without troubling ourselves to put anything valuable back into it. Since it is accidental, impersonal, we owe it nothing. We simply owe ourselves as big a share of pleasure as we can grasp and hold.

This, however, is a task in which it is easy to make mistakes. We need prudence to avoid cheating ourselves with short-lived pleasures that cost too much; wisdom to choose the simpler pleasures that cost less and last longer. Such shrewd calculation of the relative cost and worth of different pleasures is the sum and substance of the Epicurean philosophy. He who is shrewd to discern and prompt to snatch the most pleasure at least cost, as it is offered on the bargain counter of life,—he is the Epicurean sage.

We might work this out into a great variety of applications: but one or two spheres must suffice. Eating and drinking, as the most elemental relations of life, are the ones commonly chosen as applications of the Epicurean principle. These applications, however, the selections from Epicurus and Horace have already made clear.

The Epicurean will regulate his diet, not by the immediate, trivial, short-lived pleasures of taste, though these he will by no means despise, but mainly by their permanent effects upon health. Wholesome food, and enough of it, daintily prepared and served, he will do his best to obtain. But elaborate and ostentatious feasting he will avoid, as involving too much expense and trouble, and too heavy penalties of disease and discomfort. He will find out by practical experience the quantity, quality, and variety of simple food that keeps him in perfect condition; and no enticements of sweetmeats or stimulants will divert him from the simplicity in which the most permanent pleasure is found. To eat cake and candy between meals, to sip tea at all hours, no less than to drink whiskey to the point of intoxication, are sins against the simplicity of the true Epicurean regimen.

The Epicurean will not lose an hour of needed sleep nor tolerate such an abomination as an alarm clock in his house. If he permits himself to be awakened in the morning, it will be as Thomas B. Reed used to when, as a student at Bowdoin College, he was obliged to be in chapel at six o'clock. He had the janitor call him at half-past four, in order that he might have the luxury of feeling that he had another whole hour in which to sleep, and then call him again at the last moment which would permit him to dress in time for chapel.

These things, however, we may for the most part take for granted. We do not require a philosopher to regulate our diet for us; or to put us to bed at night, and tuck us in, and hear us say our prayers. Those elementary lessons were doubtless needed in the childhood of the race. The selection from Spencer on work and play strikes closer to the problem of the modern man; and it is at this point that we all sorely need to go to school to Epicurus. Perhaps we are inclined to look down on Epicurus's ideal as a low one. Well, if it is a low ideal, it is all the more disgraceful to fall below it. And most of us do fall below it every day of our tense and restless lives. Let us test ourselves by this ideal, and answer honestly the questions it puts to us.

How many of us are slaving all day and late into the night to add artificial superfluities to the simple necessities? How many of us know how to stop working when it begins to encroach upon our health; and to cut off anxiety and worry altogether? How many of us measure the amount and intensity of our toil by our physical strength; doing what we can do healthfully, cheerfully, joyously, and leaving the rest undone, instead of straining up to the highest notch of nervous tension during early manhood and womanhood, only to break down when the life forces begin to turn against us? Every man in any position of responsibility and influence has opportunity to do the work of twenty men. How many of us in such circumstances choose the one thing we can do best, and leave the other nineteen for other people to do, or else to remain undone? How many of us have ever seriously stopped to think where the limit of healthful effort and endurance lies, unless insomnia or dyspepsia or nervous prostration have laid their heavy hands upon us and compelled us to pause? Every breakdown from avoidable causes, every stroke of work we do after the border-land of exhaustion and nervous strain is crossed, is a crime against the teaching of Epicurus; and these diseases that beset our modern business life are the penalties with which nature visits us in vindication of the wisdom of his teachings. Every day that we work beyond our strength; every hour that we spend in consequent exhaustion and depression; every minute that we give over to worrying about things beyond our immediate control, we either fall below, or else rise above, Epicurus's level.

If we rise above him, to serve higher ideals, conscious of the sacrifice we make, and clear about the superior ends we gain thereby, then we may be forgiven. What some of those higher ideals are we shall have occasion to consider later. But to work ourselves into depression, disease, and pain, for no better reason than to get high mark in some rank-book or other, to gratify somebody's false vanity, to get together a little more gold than we can spend wisely or our children can inherit without enervation, to live in a bigger house than our neighbour has or we can afford to take care of—to work for such ends as these beyond the point where work is healthy and happy, is to commit a sin which neither Epicurus nor Nature will forgive. With the people who have risen above Epicurus, and are deliberately sacrificing to some extent the Epicurean to one of the higher ideals, as I have said, we have no quarrel; for them we have only hearty commendation. We do not ask the mother whose child is dangerously sick, the statesman in a political crisis, the artist when the conception of his great work comes over him, to heed for the time being the limits of strength and the conditions of completest health. All we ask of them is that later on, when the child has recovered, when the crisis is past, when the picture is painted, they shall reverently and humbly pay to Epicurus, or to Nature whom he represents, the penalty for their sin, by a corresponding period of complete rest and relaxation. We must bear strain at times; and Nature will forgive us if we do not take it too often. But we must not bunch our strains. We must not pass from one strain to another, and another, without periods of relaxation between. We must not let the attitude of strain become chronic, and develop into a moral tetanus, which keeps us forever on the rack of exertion from sheer restless inability to sit down and enjoy ourselves.

What we take from excessive work Epicurus would bid us add to needed play. Play is an arrangement by which we get artificially, in highly concentrated form, the pleasure which in ordinary life is diffused over long periods, and attainable only in attenuated form. Play puts the great fundamental pleasures of the race at the disposal of the individual.

Foot-ball, for instance, gives the student of to-day the essential joy in combat of his barbarian ancestors, with the modern field-marshal's delight in subtle tragedy thrown in. Baseball gives the intense zest that comes of speed, accuracy, and cunning exercised in emergencies. Golf, in milder form, gives us the pleasure that comes of accuracy of aim and calculation of conditions in good company and in the open air. Billiards give to the clerk cramped all day over his desk the joy of a delicate touch which otherwise would be the exclusive property of his artisan brother. The various games of cards give the mechanic and the housewife a taste at evening of the eager interests that fill the banker's and the broker's days. Checkers and chess give to the humblest in their homes some touch of the pleasures of the general and admiral. Dancing carries to the limit of orderly expression that delight in the person and presence of the opposite sex which otherwise would have to be postponed until youth was able to assume the more serious responsibilities of permanent relationships. Sailing, tramping, camping out, hunting, fishing, mountain climbing, are all devices for bringing into the lives of studious, strenuous, city people the elemental pleasures which otherwise would be the monopoly of sailors, fishermen, foresters, and explorers. Swimming, skating, bicycle riding, driving a horse or an automobile, all give the keen joy that comes of the mastery of graceful and forceful motion.

The theatre, which embodies so distinctively the peculiar essence of play that its performances have appropriated the name, takes us in a couple of hours through the epitomised experience of many persons extending over many years in circumstances far removed from our individual lives. Poetry, novels, biographies, histories, painting, music, and all the forms of art perform for us this same function. They take us out of our local and temporal situation, and let us live in other days and other lands, in other customs and costumes; and so enormously widen the world of experience we imaginatively make our own. Besides in all the forms of play and art the ends are made artificially simple, the means are made supernaturally accessible; so that instead of toiling for years in doubt of results as in actual work, we experience in play, and witness in artistic representation, the whole process of selecting materials and moulding them to a successful issue in a few minutes, or a few hours at most. All this reacts upon our power to prosecute with confidence the remoter ends, and marshal the more obdurate means of real work. It expands and limbers our capacity to subordinate means to ends and find delight in the process as well as in the outcome. Hence a man who goes a year without a considerable period given over to play, or a week without at least one or two solid periods of it, or lets many days go by without any play whatever, is selling his birthright of personality for a mess of pottage. Psychology and pedagogy are recognising the important function of play in the development of personality as never before.

Professor Baldwin, in his *Social and Ethical Interpretations*, sums up the functions of play in these words: "In the education of the individual for his life-work in a network of social relationships play is a most important form of organic exercise,—a most important method of realisation of the social instincts; gives flexibility of mind and body with self-control; gives constant opportunity for imitative learning and invention, and is the experimental verification of the benefits and pleasures of united action."

The Epicurean price of happiness

Whoever contracts his work and expands his play, on Epicurean principles, will of course have common sense enough to cut off hurry and worry altogether. Both are sheer waste and wantonness,—the most foolish and wicked things in the whole list of forbidden sins. The Epicurean will live his life in care-tight, worry-proof compartments; working with all his might while he works; and then cutting it off short; never letting the cares of work intrude on the precious precincts of well-earned leisure, or permitting the strain of remembered or anticipated toil to mar the hours sacred to rest and recreation. Some things are bound to go wrong in every life. That is our misfortune. But there is no need of brooding over them in gratuitous grief after they have gone, or dreading them in gloomy anticipation before they come. If either in anticipation or in retrospect these evils are permitted to darken the hours when they are physically absent, that is not our misfortune; it is our folly and our fault.

We hear a great deal in these days about mind cures, and rest cures, and faith cures, and cures by hypnotism, and cures by patent medicines. If anybody needs these cures, of course he is welcome to them; though there is much to be said for the stalwart conservative who refused proffered aid of this sort with the remark that he would rather die in the hands of a skilful physician than be cured by a quack. Strict obedience to the plain, homely doctrine of Epicurus would prevent ninety-nine one hundredths of the physical and mental ailments which these various systems of healing profess to cure. In almost every such case work, or the square of work which is hurry, or the cube of work which is worry, carried beyond the sane limits which Epicurus prescribes, is at the root of trouble. Where it is not work and worry, it is their passive counterparts, grief nursed long after its occasion has gone by, or fear harboured long before its appropriate object has arrived. Cut these off and all the use you will have for either healers or physicians will be on such comparatively rare occasions as birth, death, contagious diseases, and unavoidable accident. You will not be the chronic patient of any doctor regular or irregular; or the consumer of any medicine, patented or prescribed.

Neither useless regrets for the past nor profitless forebodings for the future should ever cast their shadows over the present, which taken in itself is always endurable, and may generally be made positively happy. Memory should be purged of all its unpleasantness before its pictures are permitted to appear before the footlights of reflection; and the searchlight of expectation should always be turned toward the pleasures that are still in store for us. Past and future are mainly in our power, so far as the quality of things we remember and anticipate are concerned. And even the brief and fleeting present is mainly filled by reminiscence and anticipation, so that it too is largely what we please to make it.

> "The world is so full of a number of things,
> I'm sure we should all be as happy as kings."

If any one of us is not happy all the time, except at the rare instants when toothache, or the news of a friend's illness or death, or a bad turn in our investments takes us by surprise—if happiness is not the dominant tone of our ordinary life, it is simply because we do not want it, in that thoughtful, enterprising, insistent way in which the scholar wants knowledge, or the business man wants money, or the politician wants votes. Whoever is willing to pay the price in prudent planning of his daily pleasures, in relentless exclusion of the enterprises and indulgences that cost more pain than they can return in pleasure; whoever will cut out remorselessly the things in his past life on which he cannot dwell with pleasure, and lop off the considerations which give rise to dread; whoever is willing to pay this Epicurean price for happiness can have it just as soon and just as often as he pays down the cash of a faithful and consistent application of these principles. If any man goes about the world in a chronic unhappiness, it is ninety-nine per cent the fault, not of his circumstances, but of himself. There is not a reader of this book whose circumstances are so black that another person, in those same circumstances, would not find a way to be supremely and dominantly, if not exclusively and continuously, happy. There is not a reader of this book so rich, so blessed with family and friends, so occupied and diverted, but that another person in those same circumstances would be miserable himself, and a source of misery to everybody with whom he came in contact. Epicurus is right, that happiness is up at auction all the time, and sold in lots to suit the purchaser whenever he bids high enough. And the price is not exorbitant: prudence to plan for the simple pleasures that can be had for the asking; resolution to cut off the pleasures that come too high; determination to amputate our reflections the instant they develop morbid symptoms, and to take an anti-toxin against fret and worry, the moment we feel the approach of their contagious atmosphere; concentration, to live in a self-chosen present from which profitless regret and unprofitable anxieties, projected from the past or borrowed from the future, are absolutely banished.

It is high time to treat melancholy, depression, gloom, fretfulness, unhappiness, not merely as diseases, but as the inexcusable follies, the intolerable vices, the unpardonable sins which a sane and wholesome Epicureanism pronounces them to be.

The Epicurean principle, then, forbids us to go whining, whimpering, and weeping through this glorious and otherwise cheery world, making ourselves a burden and nuisance to our friends; and tells us frankly that if we are so much as tempted to such melancholy living, it is because we are too improvident, too slothful, too stupid to cast out these devils, which a little plain fare, hard work, outdoor exercise, vigorous play, and unworried rest would exorcise forever. It bids us put in place of these banished sighs and groans and tears, the laughter, song, and shout that "spin the great wheel of earth about." We may sum it all up in the picture of a worthy Epicurean's day.

After a night of sleep too sound to harbour an unpleasant dream, he greets the hour of rising with a shout and bound, plunges into the bath, meets with gusto the shock it gives, and rejoices in the glow of exhilaration a vigorous rubbing brings; greets the household "with morning face and morning heart," eager to share with the family the meal, the news, the outlook on the day, resolved like Pippa to "waste no wavelet of his twelve-hours' treasure"; then, whether work calls him forth immediately or not, takes a few minutes of brisk walking and deep breathing in the open air until he feels the great forces of earth, air, and sunshine pulsing in his veins; then greets the work of kitchen or factory, office or field, schoolroom or counter, bench or desk with an inward cheer, as something to put forth his surplus energy upon; and through the swift, precious forenoon hours delights in the mastery over difficulty his stored-up power imparts; takes the noon-day meal gayly and leisurely with congenial people; through the early afternoon hours does the lighter portion of the day's work if he must; gets out for an hour or two in the open air if he may, with horse, or wheel, or automobile, or boat, or racket, or golf clubs, or skates, or rod, or gun, or at least a friend and two stout walking shoes; comes to the evening meal in the family circle widened to include a few welcome guests, or at the home of some hospitable host, in garments from which all trace of stain or hint of strain has been removed, to share the best things market and purse afford, served in such wise as to prolong the opportunity for the interchange of wit and banter, cursory discussion and kindly compliment; spends the evening in quiet reading or public entertainment, games with his children or visiting with friends; and then returns again to sleep with such a sense of gratitude for the dear joys of the day as sends an echo of "All's well" down through even the shadowy substance of his unconscious dreams. Surely there are some features of this Epicurean day which we, in our bustling, restless, overelaborated lives, might introduce with great profit to ourselves, and great advantage to the people with whom we are intimately thrown. A series of such days, varied by even happier holidays and Sundays, broken once or twice a year at least by considerable vacations, added together, will make a life which Epicurus says a man may live with satisfaction, and after which he may pass away content.

If there be no other life, let us by all means make the most of this. And if, both here and hereafter, there be a larger life than that perceivable by sense,—as, on deeper grounds than the Epicurean psychology recognises, most of us believe there is,—this healthy, hearty, wholesome determination to live intensely and exclusively in the present is a much more sincere and effective way to develop it than the foolish attempt of a false other-worldliness to anticipate or discount the future, by a half-hearted, far-away affectation of superiority to the simple homely pleasures of to-day.

The defects of Epicureanism

Thus far we have pointed out certain valuable elements of truth which Epicureanism contains. Only incidentally have we encountered certain deep defects. Epicurus's "free laugh" at those who attempt to fulfil their political duties, his quiet ignoring of all interests that lie outside his little circle, or reach beyond the grave, his naïve remark about the intrinsic harmlessness of wrong-doing, provided only the wrong-doer could escape the fear of being caught, must have made us aware that there are heights of nobleness, depths of devotion, lengths of endurance, breadths of sympathy altogether foreign to this easy-going, pleasure-seeking view of life. Justice requires us to dwell more explicitly on these Epicurean shortcomings. Much that has been charged against the school in the form of swinish sensuality is the grossest slander. Still there are defects in this view of life which are both logically deducible from its premises, and practically visible in the lives of its consistent disciples.

The fundamental defect of Epicureanism is its false definition of personality. According to Epicurus the person is merely a bundle of appetites and passions; and the gratification of these is made synonymous with the satisfaction of himself. But gratifications are short; while appetites are long. The result is that which Schopenhauer has so conclusively pointed out. During the long periods when desire burns unsatisfied, the balance of pleasure is against us. In the comparatively brief and rare intervals when passions are in process of gratification, the balance can never be more than even. Therefore our account with the world at the end of any period, whether a week or a year or a lifetime, is bound to stand as follows: credit, a few rare, brief moments—moments, too, which have long since vanished into nothingness—when appetites and passions were in process of satisfaction. Debit, the vast majority of moments, amounting in the aggregate to almost the total period considered, when appetites and passions were clamouring for a satisfaction that was not forthcoming. The obvious conclusion from the frequent examination of the Epicurean account-book is that which Schopenhauer so triumphantly demonstrates,—pessimism. The sooner we cease doing business on those terms, the less will be the balance of pain, or unsatisfied desire, against us. To be entirely frank, the devotees of Omar Khayyam would have to confess that it is this note of pessimism, despair, and self-pity, at the sorry contrast of the vast unattainable and the petty attained, which is the secret of his unquestionably fascinating lines. Here the blasé amusement-seeker finds consolation in the fact that a host of other people are also yielding to the temptation to bury the unwelcome consciousness of a self they cannot satisfy in wine, or any other momentary sensuous titillation that will conceal the sense of their spiritual failure—a failure, however, which they are glad to be assured is shared by so many that the sense of it has been dignified by the name of a philosophy and sung by a poet.

Pleasure cannot be sought directly with success; for pleasure comes indirectly as the effect of causes far higher and deeper and wider than any that are recognised in the Epicurean philosophy. Pleasure comes unsought to those who lose themselves in large intellectual, artistic, social, and spiritual interests. But such noble losing of self without thought of gain is explicitly excluded from the consistent Epicurean creed.

In the picture of the Epicurean life already drawn, while domestic and political life have been presupposed as a background, nothing has been said about the sacrifice which one is called upon to make in the support and defence of a pure home and a free country. That was expressly excluded by Epicurus. Whatever attractiveness there was in the picture of the Epicurean life previously presented was largely due to this background of presupposition that this happy life was lived in a well-ordered and stable family, and in a free and just municipal and national life. In fact it is only as a parasite on these great domestic, social, and political institutions which it does nothing to create or maintain, and much to weaken and destroy, that Epicureanism is even a tolerable account of life. If we now paint our picture of the Epicurean man and woman with this background of domestic and civic life withdrawn, the ugliness and meanness of this parasitic Epicureanism will stare us in the face; and while we ought not to forget the valuable lessons it has to teach us, we shall shrink from the completed picture as a thing of deformity and degradation.

Who then is the consistent Epicurean man? He is the club man, who lives in easy luxury and fares sumptuously every day. Everything is done for him. Servants wait on him. He serves nobody, and is responsible for no one's welfare. He has a congenial set of cronies, loosely attached to be sure; and constantly changing, as matrimony, financial reverses, business engagements, professional responsibilities call one or another of his circle away to a more strenuous life. He is a good fellow, genial, free-handed with his set, indifferent to all who are outside. He generally hires some woman to serve for a few months as the instrument of his passions; only to cast her off to be hired by another and another until in due time she dies, he cares not when or how.

As business men these Epicureans are apt to be easy-going, and therefore failures. As debtors, they are the hardest people in the world from whom to collect a bill. As creditors or landlords they are the most merciless in their exactions. Their devotion to the state is generally confined to betting on the elections; the returns of which they watch with the same interest as the results of a horse-race. Their religion is confined to poking fun at the people who are foolish enough to be going to church while they are at their Sunday morning breakfast.

We all know these Epicureans; we do business with them; we meet them socially; we treat them decently; but it is to be hoped that underneath the smooth exterior we all detect their selfish heartlessness. They have taken a doctrine, which, as applied to the good things which are made to minister to our appetites is sound and true, and have perverted it into a moral monstrosity by daring to treat human hearts and social institutions as mere things, mere instruments of their selfish pleasures.

Epicurean women, likewise, abound in every wealthy community. They spend the winter in Florida, New York, or Washington; dividing the rest of the year between the sea-shore, the mountains, and the lakes, with occasional visits to what they call their homes. They must have the best of everything, and assume no responsibility beyond running up bills for their husbands to pay, or to remain unpaid. Their special paradise is foreign travel, and no pension or hotel along the beaten highways of Europe is without its quota of these precious daughters of Epicurus. They flit hither and thither where least ennui and most diversion allures. Two or three years of this irresponsible existence is sufficient to disqualify them for usefulness either in Europe or America, either here or hereafter. When they return, if they ever do, to their native town or city, the drudgery of housekeeping has become intolerable, the responsibilities of social life unendurable, and their poor husbands are glad enough when the restless fit seizes them again and they can be packed off to Egypt, or Russia, or whatever remote corner of the earth remains for their idle hands and restless feet, their empty minds and hollow hearts, to invade with their unearned gold.

There is no guarantee that the Epicurean will be the chaste husband of one wife, or a faithful mother, or a good provider for the family, or a devoted citizen of the republic, or a strenuous servant of art or science, or a heroic martyr in the cause of progress and reform. If all men were Epicureans, the world would speedily retrograde into the barbarism and animalism whence it has slowly and painfully emerged. The great interests of the family, the state, society, and civilisation are not accurately reflected in the feelings of the individual; and if the individual has no guide but feeling, he will prove a traitor to such of these higher interests as may have the misfortune to be intrusted to his pleasure-loving, self-indulgent, unheroic hands.

There are hard things to do and to endure; and if we are to meet them bravely, we shall have to call the Stoic to our aid. There are sordid and trivial things to put up with, or to rise above, and there we may need at times the Platonist and the mystic to show us the eternal reality underneath the temporal appearance. There are problems of conduct to be solved; conflicting claims to be adjusted; and for this the Aristotelian sense of proportion must be developed in our souls. Finally there are other persons to be considered, and one great Personal Spirit living and working in the world; and for our proper attitude toward these persons, human and divine, we must look to the Christian principle. To meet these higher relationships with no better equipment than Epicureanism offers, would be as foolish as to try to run barefoot across a continent, or swim naked across the sea. Naked, barefoot Epicureanism has its place on the sandy beaches and in the sheltered coves of life; but has no business on the mountain tops or in the depths of human experience.

It will not make a man an efficient workman, or a thorough scholar, or a brave soldier, or a public-spirited citizen. It spoils completely every woman whom it gets hold of, unless at the same time she has firm hold on something better; unless she has a husband and children whom she loves, or work in which she delights for its own sake, or friends and interests dearer than life itself. Epicureanism will not lift either man or woman far toward heaven, or save them in the hour when the pains of hell get hold of them. No home can be reared on it. The divorce court is the logical outcome of every marriage between a man and a woman who are both Epicureans. For it is the very essence of Epicureanism to treat others as means; while no marriage is tolerable unless at least one of the two parties is large and unselfish enough to treat the other as an end. No Epicurean state or city could endure longer than it would take for the men who are in politics for their pockets to plunder the people who are out of politics for the same reason. An Epicurean heaven, a place where eternally each should get his fill of pleasure at the expense of everybody else, would be insufferably insipid, incomparably unendurable. It is fortunate for the fame of Epicurus and the permanence of his philosophy that he evaded the necessity of thinking out the conditions of immortal blessedness by his specious dilemma in which he thought to prove that death ends all. As a temporary parasite upon a political and moral order already established, Epicureanism might thrive and flourish; but as a principle on which to rest a decent society here or a hope of heaven hereafter, Epicureanism is utterly lacking. If there were nothing better than Epicureanism in store for us through the long eternities, we all might well pray to be excused, as Epicurus happily believed we should be. For any ultimate delight in life must be rooted in something deeper than self-centred pleasure: it must love persons and seek ends for their own sake; and find its joy, not in the satisfaction of the man as he is, but in the development of that which his thought and love enable him to become.

An example of Epicurean character

The clearest example of the shortcomings of Epicureanism is the character of Tito Melema in George Eliot's *Romola*. Pleasure and the avoidance of pain are this young Greek's only principles. He is "of so easy a conscience that he would make a stepping-stone of his father's corpse."

"He has a lithe sleekness about him that seems marvellously fitted for slipping into any nest he fixes his mind on."

"He had an unconquerable aversion to any thing unpleasant, even when an object very much loved and admired was on the other side of it."

According to his thinking "any maxims that required a man to fling away the good that was needed to make existence sweet, were only the lining of human selfishness turned outward; they were made by men who wanted others to sacrifice themselves for their sake."

"He would rather that Baldassarre should not suffer; he liked no one to suffer; but could any philosophy prove to him that he was bound to care for another's suffering more than for his own? To do so, he must have loved Baldassarre devotedly, and he did not love him: was that his own fault? Gratitude! seen closely, it made no valid claim; his father's life would have been dreary without him; are we convicted of a debt to men for the pleasure they give themselves?"

"He had simply chosen to make life easy to himself—to carry his human lot if possible in such a way that it should pinch him nowhere; but the choice had at various times landed him in unexpected positions."

"Tito could not arrange life at all to his mind without a considerable sum of money, and that problem of arranging life to his mind had been the source of all his misdoing."

"He would have been equal to any sacrifice that was not unpleasant."

"Of other goods than pleasure he can form no conception."

As Romola says in her reproaches: "You talk of substantial good, Tito! Are faithfulness, and love, and sweet grateful memories no good? Is it no good that we should keep our silent promises on which others build because they believe in our love and truth? Is it no good that a just life should be justly honoured? Or, is it good that we should harden our hearts against all the wants and hopes of those who have depended on us? What good can belong to men who have such souls? To talk cleverly, perhaps, and find soft couches for themselves, and live and die with their base selves as their best companions."

This pleasure-loving Tito Melema, "when he was only seven years old, Baldassarre had rescued from blows, had taken to a home that seemed like opened paradise, where there was sweet food and soothing caresses, all had on Baldassarre's knee; and from that time till the hour they had parted, Tito had been the one centre of Baldassarre's fatherly cares."

Instead of finding and rescuing this man who, long years ago, had rescued Tito when a little boy from a life of beggary, filth, and cruel wrong, had reared him tenderly and been to him as a father, Tito sold the jewels which belonged to his father and would have been sufficient to ransom him from slavery, and finally, when found by Baldassarre in Florence, denied him and pronounced him a madman. He betrayed an innocent, trusting young girl into a mock marriage, at the same time ruining her and proving false to his lawful wife. He sold the library which it was Romola's father's dying wish to have kept in Florence as a distinct memorial to his life and work. He entered into selfish intrigues in the politics of the city, ready to betray his associates and friends whenever his own safety required it.

What wonder that Romola came to have "her new scorn of that thing called pleasure which made men base—that dexterous contrivance for selfish ease, that shrinking from endurance and strain, when others were bowing beneath burdens too heavy for them, which now made one image with her husband." In her own distress she learns from Savonarola that there is a higher law than individual pleasure. "She felt that the sanctity attached to all close relations, and therefore preëminently to the closest, was but the expression in outward law, of that result toward which all human goodness and nobleness must spontaneously tend; that the light abandonment of ties, whether inherited or voluntary, because they had ceased to be pleasant, was the uprooting of social and personal virtue. What else had Tito's crime toward Baldassarre been but that abandonment working itself out to the most hideous extreme of falsity and ingratitude? To her, as to him, there had come one of those moments in life when the soul must dare to act on its own warrant, not only without external law to appeal to, but in the face of a law which is not unarmed with Divine lightnings—lightnings that may yet fall if the warrant has been false." The whole teaching of the book is summed up in the Epilogue. In the conversation between Romola and Tito's illegitimate son Lillo, Lillo says, "I should like to be something that would make me a great man, and very happy besides—something that would not hinder me from having a good deal of pleasure."

"That is not easy, my Lillo. It is only a poor sort of happiness that could ever come by caring very much about our own narrow pleasures. We can only have the highest happiness, such as goes along with being a great man, by having wide thoughts, and much feeling for the rest of the world as well as ourselves; and this sort of happiness often brings so much pain with it, that we can only tell it from pain by its being what we would choose before everything else, because our souls see it is good. There are so many things wrong and difficult in the world, that no man can be great—he can hardly keep himself from wickedness—unless he gives up thinking much about pleasure or rewards, and gets strength to endure what is hard and painful. My father had the greatness that belongs to integrity; he chose poverty and obscurity rather than falsehood. And there was Fra Girolamo—you know why I keep to-morrow sacred; he had the greatness which belongs to a life spent in struggling against powerful wrong, and in trying to raise men to the highest deeds they are capable of. And so, my Lillo, if you mean to act nobly and seek to know the best things God has put within reach of men, you must learn to fix your mind on that end, and not on what will happen to you because of it. And remember, if you were to choose something lower, and make it the rule of your life to seek your own pleasure, and escape from what is disagreeable, calamity might come just the same; and it would be calamity falling on a base mind, which is the one form of sorrow that has no balm in it, and that may well make a man say, 'It would have been better for me if I had never been born.'"

The trouble with Epicureanism is its assumption that the self is a bundle of natural appetites and passions, and that the end of life is their gratification. Experience shows, as in the case of Tito, that such a policy consistently pursued, brings not pleasure but pain—pain first of all to others, and then pain to the individual through their contempt, indignation, and vengeance. The truest pleasure must come through the development within one of generous emotions, kind sympathies, and large social interests. The man must be made over before the pleasures of the new man can be rightly sought and successfully found. This making over of man is no consistent part of the logical Epicurean programme, and consequently pure Epicureanism is sure to land one in the narrowness, selfishness, and heartlessness of a Tito Melema, and to bring upon one essentially the same condemnation and disaster.

Still, not in criticism or unkindness would we take leave of the serene and genial Epicurus. We may frankly recognise his fundamental limitations, and yet gratefully accept the good counsel he has to give. Parasite as it is,— a thing that can only live by sucking its life out of ideals and principles higher and hardier than itself, it is yet a graceful and ornamental parasite, which will beautify and shield the hard outlines of our more strenuous principles. There are dreary wastes in all our lives, into which we can profitably turn those streams of simple pleasure he commends. There are points of undue strain and tension where Epicurean prudence would bid us forego the slight fancied gain to save the ruinous expense to health and happiness. Let us fill up these gaps with hearty indulgence of healthy appetite, with vigorous exercise of dormant powers, with the eager joys of new-learned recreations. Let us tone down the strain and tension of our anxious, worried, worn, and weary lives by the rigid elimination of the superfluous, the strict concentration on the perpetual present, the resolute banishment from it of all past or future springs of depression and discouragement. Before we are through we shall see far nobler ideals than this; but we must not despise the day of small things. Though the lowest and least of them all, the Epicurean is one of the historical ideals of life. It has its claims which none of us may with impunity ignore. To serve him faithfully in the lower spheres of life is a wholesome preparation for the intelligent and reasonable service of Stoic, Platonic, Aristotelian, and Christian ideals which rule the higher realms. He who is false to the humble, homely demands of Epicurus can never be quite at his best in the grander service of Zeno and Plato, Aristotle and Jesus.

The Confessions of an Epicurean Heretic

A heretic is a man who, while professing to hold the tenets of the sect to which he adheres, and sincerely believing that he is in substantial agreement with his more orthodox brethren, yet in his desire to be honest and reasonable, so modifies these tenets as to empty them of all that is distinctive of the sect in question, and thus unintentionally gives aid and comfort to its enemies. Every vigorous and vital school of thought soon or late develops this species of enfant terrible. Like the Christian church, the Epicurean school has been blessed with numerous progeny of this disturbing sort. The one among them all who most stoutly professes the fundamental principles of Epicureanism, and then proceeds to admit pretty much everything its opponents advance against it, is John Stuart Mill. His "Utilitarianism" is a fort manned with the most approved idealistic guns, yet with the Epicurean flag floating bravely over the whole. He "holds that actions are right in proportion as they tend to promote happiness, wrong as they tend to produce the reverse of happiness. By happiness is intended pleasure and the absence of pain; by unhappiness, pain and the privation of pleasure. Pleasure and freedom from pain are the only things desirable as ends; and all desirable things are desirable either for the pleasure inherent in themselves, or as means to the promotion of pleasure and the prevention of pain." A more square and uncompromising statement of Epicureanism than this it would be impossible to make.

Having thus squarely identified himself with the Epicurean school, Mr. Mill proceeds to add to this doctrine in turn the doctrines of each one of the four schools which we are to consider later. First he introduces a distinction in the kind of pleasure, "assigning to the pleasures of the intellect, of the feelings and imagination, and of the moral sentiments, a much higher value as pleasures than to those of mere sensation." When asked what he means by difference of quality in pleasures, or what makes one pleasure more valuable than another, merely as a pleasure, except its being greater in amount, although he tells us there is but one possible answer, he gives us two or three.

First he appeals to the verdict of competent judges.

"Of two pleasures, if there be one to which all or almost all who have experience of both give a decided preference, irrespective of any feeling of moral obligation to prefer it, that is the more desirable pleasure. If one of the two is, by those who are competently acquainted with both, placed so far above the other that they prefer it, even though knowing it to be attended with a greater amount of discontent, and would not resign it for any quantity of the other pleasure which their nature is capable of, we are justified in ascribing to the preferred enjoyment a superiority in quality, so far outweighing quantity as to render it, in comparison, of small account."

This appeal to competent judges, or, in other words, to authority, involves no philosophical principle at all unless we may call the doctrine of papal infallibility, to which this appeal of Mill is essentially akin, a principle. If these judges are competent, there must be a reason for the preference they give. In the next paragraph Mill tells us what that principle is; but in doing so introduces the principle of the subordination of lower to higher faculties, which we shall see later is the distinguishing principle of Plato. On this point Mill is as clear as Plato himself. "Now it is an unquestionable fact that those who are equally acquainted with, and equally capable of appreciating and enjoying both, do give a most marked preference to the manner of existence which employs their higher faculties. Few human creatures would consent to be changed into any of the lower animals, for a promise of the fullest allowance of a beast's pleasures; no intelligent human being would consent to be a fool, no instructed person would be an ignoramus, no person of feeling and conscience would be selfish and base, even though they should be persuaded that the fool, the dunce, or the rascal is better satisfied with his lot than they are with theirs. They would not resign what they possess more than he, for the most complete satisfaction of all the desires which they have in common with him. If they ever fancy they would, it is only in cases of unhappiness so extreme, that to escape from it they would exchange their lot for almost any other, however undesirable in their own eyes. A being of higher faculties requires more to make him happy, is capable probably of more acute suffering, and is certainly accessible to it at more points, than one of an inferior type; but in spite of these liabilities, he can never really wish to sink into what he feels to be a lower grade of existence." This appeal to quality rather than quantity of pleasure puts Mill, in

38

spite of himself, squarely on Platonic ground and abandons consistent Epicureanism. An illustration will make this clear. A man professes that money is his supreme end, the only thing he cares for in the world; he tells us that whatever he does is done for money, and whenever he refrains from doing anything it is to avoid losing money. So far he puts his conduct on a consistently mercenary basis. Suppose, however, that in the next sentence he tells us that he prizes certain kinds of money. If we ask him what is the basis of the distinction, he replies that he prizes money honestly earned and despises money dishonestly acquired. Should we not at once recognise, that in spite of his original declaration, he is not the consistently mercenary being he professed himself to be? The fact that he prefers honest to dishonest money shows that honesty, not money, is his real principle; and, in spite of his original profession, this distinction lifts him out of the class of mercenary money lovers into the class of men whose real principle is not money but honesty. Precisely so Mill's confession that he cares for the height and dignity of the faculties employed rather than the quantity of pleasure gained lifts him out of the Epicurean school to which he professes adherence and makes him an idealist.

When asked for an explanation of his preference of higher to lower, Mill at once shifts to Stoic ground in the following sentences: "We may give what explanation we please of this unwillingness; we may attribute it to pride, a name which is given indiscriminately to some of the most and to some of the least estimable feelings of which mankind are capable; we may refer it to the love of liberty and personal independence, an appeal to which was with the Stoics one of the most effective means for the inculcation of it; to the love of power, or to the love of excitement, both of which do really enter into and contribute to it; but its most appropriate appellation is a sense of dignity, which all human beings possess in one form or another, and in some, though by no means in exact, proportion to their highest faculties, and which is so essential a part of the happiness of those in whom it is strong, that nothing which conflicts with it could be, otherwise than momentarily, an object of desire to them. Whoever supposes that this preference takes place at a sacrifice of happiness—that the superior being, in anything like equal circumstances, is not happier than the inferior—confounds the two very different ideas of happiness and content. It is indisputable that the being whose capacities of enjoyment are low has the greatest chance of having them fully satisfied; and a highly endowed being will always feel that any happiness which we can look for, as the world is constituted, is imperfect. But he can learn to bear its imperfections if they are at all bearable; and they will not make him envy the being who is indeed unconscious of the imperfections, but only because he feels not at all the good which those imperfections qualify. It is better to be a human being dissatisfied than a pig satisfied; better to be Socrates dissatisfied than a fool satisfied. And if the fool, or the pig, is of a different opinion, it is because they only know their own side of the question. The other party to the comparison knows both sides."

When pressed for a sanction of motive Mill appeals to the Aristotelian principle that the individual can only realise his conception of himself through union with his fellows in society: to the social nature of man and his inability to find himself in any smaller sphere, or through devotion to any lesser end. "This firm foundation is that of the social feelings of mankind; the desire to be in unity with our fellow-creatures, which is already a powerful principle in human nature, and happily one of those which tend to become stronger, even without express inculcation, from the influences of advancing civilisation. The social state is at once so natural, so necessary, and so habitual to man, that, except in some unusual circumstances or by an effort of voluntary abstraction, he never conceives himself otherwise than as a member of a body; and this association is riveted more and more, as mankind are farther removed from the state of savage independence. Any condition, therefore, which is essential to a state of society, becomes more and more an inseparable part of every person's conception of the state of things which he is born into, and which is the destiny of a human being. In this way people grow up unable to conceive as possible to them a state of total disregard of other people's interests. They are under a necessity of conceiving themselves as at least abstaining from all the grosser injuries, and (if only for their own protection) living in a state of constant protest against them. They are also familiar with the fact of coöperating with others, and proposing to themselves a collective, not an individual, interest, as the aim (at least for the time being) of their actions. So long as they are coöperating, their ends are identified with those of others; there is at least a temporary feeling that the interests of others are their own interests. Not only does all strengthening of social ties, and all healthy growth of society, give to each individual a stronger personal interest in practically consulting the welfare of others; it also leads him to identify his feelings more and more with their good, or at least with an ever greater degree of practical consideration for it. He comes, as though instinctively, to be conscious of himself as a being who of course pays regard to others. The good of others becomes to him a thing naturally and necessarily to be attended to. This mode of conceiving ourselves and human life, as civilisation goes on, is felt to be more and more natural. Every step in political improvement renders it more so by removing the sources of opposition of interest, and levelling those inequalities of legal privilege between individuals or classes, owing to which there are large portions of mankind whose happiness it is still practicable to disregard. In an improving state of the human mind, the influences are constantly on the increase, which tend to generate in each individual a feeling of unity with all the rest; which feeling, if perfect, would make him never think of, or desire, any beneficial condition for himself, in the benefits of which they are not included. The deeply rooted conception which every individual even now has of himself as a social being tends to make him feel it one of his natural wants that there should be harmony between his feelings and aims and those of his fellow-creatures. It does not present itself to their minds as a superstition of education, or a law despotically imposed by the power of society, but as an attribute which it would not be well for them to be without."

Lastly Mill introduces the Christian ideal. "As between his own happiness and that of others, utilitarianism requires him to be as strictly impartial as a disinterested and benevolent spectator. In the golden rule of Jesus of Nazareth, we read the complete spirit of the ethics of utility. To do as one would be done by, and to love one's neighbour as one's self, constitute the ideal perfection of utilitarian morality." In his attempt to prove the Christian obligation on an Epicurean basis the inconsistency between his Epicurean principle and his Christian preaching and practice becomes evident. Master of logic as Mill was, an author of a standard text-book on the subject, yet so desperate was the plight in which his attempt to stretch Epicureanism to Christian dimensions placed him, that he was compelled to resort to the following fallacy of composition, the fallaciousness of which every student of logic recognises at a glance. "Happiness is a good; each person's happiness is a good to that person, and the general happiness, therefore, a good to the aggregate of all persons." As Carlyle has pointed out, this is equivalent to saying, since each pig wants all the swill in the trough for itself, a litter of pigs in the aggregate will desire each member of the litter to have its share of the whole,—a fallacy which a single experience in feeding pigs will sufficiently refute. It requires something deeper and higher than Epicurean principles to lift men to a plane where Christian altruism is the natural and inevitable conduct which Mill rightly says it ought to be.

These confessions of an Epicurean heretic, wrung from a man who had been rigidly trained by a stern father in Epicurean principles, yet whose surpassing candour compelled him to make these admissions, so fatal to the system, so ennobling to the man and to the doctrine he proclaimed, serve as an admirable preparation for the succeeding chapters, where these same principles, which Mill introduces as supplements, and modifications, and amendments to Epicureanism, will be presented as the foundation-stones of larger and deeper views of life. Mill starts with a jack-knife which he publicly proclaims to be in every part of the handle and in every blade through and through Epicurean; then gets a new handle from the Stoics; borrows one blade from Plato, and another from Aristotle; unconsciously steals the biggest blade of all from Christianity; makes one of the best knives to be found on the moral market: yet still, in loyalty to early parental training, insists on calling the finished product by the same name as that with which he started out. The result is a splendid knife to cut with; but a difficult one to classify. Our quest for the principles of personality will not bring us anything much better, for practical purposes, than the lofty teaching of Mill's "Utilitarianism," and its companion in inconsistency, Herbert Spencer's Principles of Ethics. All our five principles are present in these so-called hedonistic treatises. But it is a great theoretical advantage, and ultimately carries with it considerable practical gain, to give credit where credit is due, and to call things by their right names. Thanks to the candour of these heretics, though the names we encounter hereafter will be new, we shall greet most of the principles we discover under these new names as old friends to whom the Epicurean heretics gave us our first introduction.

Epicurus by Charles Bradlaugh

Epicurean.—*One who holds the principles of Epicurus—Luxurious, contributing to luxury.*

Epicurism—*The principles of Epicurus—Luxury, sensual enjoyment, gross pleasure.*

The words with which this page is headed may be found in the current and established dictionaries of the present day; and it shall be our task to show that never was slander more foul, calumny more base, or libel more cowardly, than when it associated the words luxury and sensuality with the memory of the Athenian Epicurus. The much-worn anecdote of the brief endorsed "The Defendant has no case, abuse the Plaintiffs Solicitor," will well apply here. The religionists had no case, the Epicurean Philosophy was impregnable as far as theological attacks were concerned, and the theologians have, therefore, constantly and vehemently abused its founder; so that, at last, children have caught the cry as though it were the enunciation of a tact, and have grown into men believing that Epicurus was a sort of discriminating hog, who wallowed in the filth which some have miscalled pleasure.

Epicurus was born in the early part of the year 344, B. C, the third year of the 109th Olympiad, at Gargettus, in the neighborhood of Athens. His father, Neocles, was of the Aegean tribe. Some allege that Epicurus was born in the island of Samos; but, according to others, he was taken there when very young by his parents, who formed a portion of a colony of Athenian citizens, sent to colonize Samos after its subjugation by Pericles. The father and mother of Epicurus were in very humble circumstances; his father was a schoolmaster, and his mother, Chaerestrata, acted as a kind of priestess, curing diseases, exorcising ghosts, and exercising other fabulous powers. Epicurus has been charged with sorcery, because he wrote several songs for his mother's solemn rites. Until eighteen, he remained at Samos and the neighboring isle of Teos; from whence he removed to Athens, where he resided until the death of Alexander, when, disturbances arising, he fled to Colophon. This place, Mitylene, and Lampsacus, formed the philosopher's residence until he was thirty-six years of age; at which time he founded a school in the neighborhood of Athens. He purchased a pleasant garden, where he taught his disciples until the time of his death.

We are told by Laertius, "That those disciples who were regularly admitted into the school of Epicurus, lived together, not in the manner of the Pythagoreans, who cast their possessions into a common stock; for this, in his opinion, implied mutual distrust rather than friendship; but upon such a footing of friendly attachment, that each individual cheerfully supplied the necessities of his brother."

The habits of the philosopher and his followers were temperate and exceedingly frugal, and formed a strong contrast to the luxurious, although refined, manners of the Athenians. At the entrance of the garden, the visitor of Epicurus found the following inscription:—"The hospitable keeper of this mansion, where you will find pleasure the highest good, will present you with barley cakes and water from the spring. These gardens will not provoke your appetite by artificial dainties, but satisfy it with natural supplies. Will you not, then, be well entertained?" And yet the owner of the garden, over the gate of which these words were placed, has been called "a glutton" and "a stomach worshipper!"

From the age of thirty-six until his decease, he does not seem to have quitted Athens, except temporarily. When Demetrius besieged Athens, the Epicureans were driven into great difficulties for want of food; and it is said that Epicurus and his friends subsisted on a small quantity of beans which he possessed, and which he shared equally with them.

The better to prosecute his studies, Epicurus lived a life of celibacy. Temperate and continent himself, he taught his followers to be so likewise, both by example and precept. He died 273 B. C, in the seventy-third year of his age; and, at that time, his warmest opponents seem to have paid the highest compliments to his personal character; and, on reading his life, and the detailed accounts of his teachings, it seems difficult to imagine what has induced the calumny which has been heaped upon his memory.

We "cannot quote from his own works, in his own words, because, although he wrote very much, only a summary of his writings has come to us uninjured; but his doctrines have been so fully investigated and treated on, both by his opponents and his disciples, that there is no difficulty or doubt as to the principles inculcated in the school of Epicurus.

"The sum of his doctrine concerning philosophy, in general, is this:— Philosophy is the exercise of reason in the pursuit and attainment of a happy life; whence it follows, that those studies which conduce neither to the acquisition nor the enjoyment of happiness are to be dismissed as of no value. The end of all speculation ought to be, to enable men to judge with certainty what is to be chosen, and what is to be avoided, to preserve themselves free from pain, and to secure health of body, and tranquillity of mind. True philosophy is so useful to every man, that the young should apply to it without delay, and the old should never be weary of the pursuit; for no man is either too young or too old to correct and improve his mind, and to study the art of happiness. Happy are they who possess by nature a free and vigorous intellect, and who are born in a country where they can prosecute their inquiries without restraint: for it is philosophy alone which raises a man above vain fears and base passions, and gives him the perfect command of himself. As nothing ought to be dearer to a philosopher than truth, he should, pursue it by the most direct means, devising no actions himself, nor suffering himself to be imposed upon by the fictions of others, neither poets, orators, nor logicians, making no other use of the rules of rhetoric or grammar, than to enable him to speak or write with accuracy and perspicuity, and always preferring a plain and simple to an ornamented style. Whilst some doubt of everything, and others profess to acknowledge everything, a wise man will embrace such tenets, and only such as are built upon experience, or upon certain and indisputable axioms."

The following is a summary of his Moral Philosophy:—

"The end of living, or the ultimate good, which is to be sought for its own sake, according to the universal opinion of mankind, is happiness; yet men, for the most part, fail in the pursuit of this end, either because they do not form a right idea of the nature of happiness, or because they do not make use of proper means to attain it. Since it is every man's interest to be happy through the whole of life, it is the wisdom of every one to employ philosophy in the search of felicity without delay; and there cannot be a greater folly, than to be always beginning to live.

"The happiness which belongs to man, is that state in which he enjoys as many of the good things, and suffers as few of the evils incident to human nature as possible; passing his days in a smooth course of permanent tranquillity. A wise man, though deprived of sight or hearing, may experience happiness in the enjoyment of the good things which yet remain; and when suffering torture, or laboring under some painful disease, can mitigate the anguish by patience, and can enjoy, in his afflictions, the consciousness of his own constancy. But it is impossible that perfect happiness can be possessed without the pleasure which attends freedom from pain, and the enjoyment of the good things of life. Pleasure is in its nature good, as pain is in its nature evil; the one is, therefore, to be pursued, and the other to be avoided, for its own sake.—Pleasure, or pain, is not only good, or evil, in itself, but the measure of what is good or evil, in every object of desire or aversion; for the ultimate reason why we pursue one thing, and avoid another, is because we expect pleasure from the former, and apprehend pain from the latter. If we sometimes decline a present pleasure, it is not because we are averse to pleasure itself, but because we conceive, that in the present instance, it will be necessarily connected with a greater pain. In like manner, if we sometimes voluntarily submit to a present pain, it is because we judge that it is necessarily connected with a greater pleasure.—Although all pleasure is essentially good, and all pain essentially evil, it doth not thence necesnecessarily follow, that in every single instance the one ought to be pursued, and the other to be avoided; but reason is to be employed in distinguishing and comparing the nature and degrees of each, that the result may be a wise choice of that which shall appear to be, upon the whole, good. That pleasure is the first good, appears from the inclination which every animal, from its first birth, discovers to pursue pleasure, and avoid pain; and is confirmed by the universal experience of mankind, who are incited to action by no other principle than the desire of avoiding pain, or obtaining pleasure. There are two kinds of pleasure: one consisting in a state of rest, in which both body and mind are undisturbed by any kind of pain; the other arising from an agreeable agitation of the senses, producing a correspondent emotion in the soul. It is upon the former of these that the enjoyment of life chiefly depends. Happiness may therefore be said to consist in bodily ease, and mental tranquillity, When pleasure is asserted to be the end of living, we are not then to understand that violent kind of delight or joy which arises from the gratification of the senses and passions, but merely that placid state of mind, which results from the absence of every cause of pain or uneasiness. Those pleasures, which arise from agitation, are not to be pursued as in themselves the end of living, but as means of arriving at that stable tranquillity, in which true happiness consists. It is the office of reason to confine the pursuit of pleasure within the limits of nature, in order to the attainment of that happy state, in which the body is free from every kind of pain, and the mind from all perturbation. This state must not, however, be conceived to be perfect in proportion as it is inactive and torpid, but in proportion as all the functions of life are quietly and pleasantly performed. A happy life neither resembles a rapid torrent, nor a standing pool, but is like a gentle stream, that glides smoothly and silently along.

"This happy state can only be obtained by a prudent care of the body, and a steady government of the mind. The diseases of the body are to be prevented by temperance, or cured by medicine, or rendered tolerable by patience. Against the diseases of the mind, philosophy provides sufficient antidotes. The instruments which it employs for this purpose are the virtues; the root of which, whence all the rest proceed, is prudence. This virtue comprehends the whole art of living discreetly, justly, and honorably, and is, in fact, the same thing with wisdom. It instructs men to free their understandings from the clouds of prejudice; to exercise temperance and fortitude in the government of themselves: and to practice justice towards others. Although pleasure, or happiness, which is the end of living, be superior to virtue, which is only the means, it is every one's interest to practice all the virtues; for in a happy life, pleasure can never be separated from virtue.

"A prudent man, in order to secure his tranquillity, will consult his natural disposition in the choice of his plan of life. If, for example, he be persuaded that he should be happier in a state of marriage than in celibacy, he ought to marry; but if he be convinced that matrimony would be an impediment to his happiness, he ought to remain single. In like manner, such persons as are naturally active, enterprising, and ambitious, or such as by the condition of their birth are placed in the way of civil offices, should accommodate themselves to their nature and situation, by engaging in public affairs; while such as are, from natural temper, fond of leisure and retirement, or, from experience or observation, are convinced that a life of public business would be inconsistent with their happiness, are unquestionably at liberty, except where particular circumstances call them to the service of their country, to pass their lives in obscure repose.

"Temperance is that discreet regulation of the desires and passions, by which we are enabled to enjoy pleasures without suffering any consequent inconvenience. They who maintain such a constant self-command, as never to be enticed by the prospect of present indulgence, to do that which will be productive of evil, obtain the truest pleasure by declining pleasure. Since, of desires some are natural and necessary; others natural, but not necessary; and others neither natural nor necessary, but the offspring of false judgment; it must be the office of temperance to gratify the first class, as far as nature requires: to restrain the second within the bounds of moderation; and, as to the third, resolutely to oppose, and, if possible, entirely repress them.

"Sobriety, as opposed to inebriety and gluttony, is of admirable use in teaching men that nature is satisfied with a little, and enabling them to content themselves with simple and frugal fare. Such a manner of living is conducive to the preservation of health: renders a man alert and active in all the offices of life; affords him an exquisite relish of the occasional varieties of a plentiful board, and prepares him to meet every reverse of fortune without the fear of want.

"Continence is a branch of temperance, which prevents the diseases, infamy, remorse, and punishment, to which those are exposed, who indulge themselves in unlawful amours. Music and poetry, which are often employed as incentives to licentious pleasure are to be cautiously and sparingly used.

"Gentleness, as opposed to an irascible temper, greatly contributes to the tranquillity and happiness of life, by preserving the mind from perturbation, and arming it against the assaults of calumny and malice. A wise man, who puts himself under the government of reason, will be able to receive an injury with calmness, and to treat the person who committed it with lenity; for he will rank injuries among the casual events of life, and will prudently reflect that he can no more stop the natural current of human passions, than he can curb the stormy winds. Refractory servants in a family should be chastised, and disorderly members of a state punished without wrath.

"Moderation, in the pursuit of honors or riches, is the only security against disappointment and vexation. A wise man, therefore, will prefer the simplicity of rustic life to the magnificence of courts. Future events a wise man will consider as uncertain, and will, therefore, neither suffer himself to be elated with confident expectation, nor to be depressed by doubt and despair: for both are equally destructive of tranquillity. It will contribute to the enjoyment of life, to consider death as the perfect termination of a happy life, which it becomes us to close like satisfied guests, neither regretting the past, nor anxious for the future.

"Fortitude, the virtue which enables us to endure pain, and to banish fear, is of great use in producing tranquillity. Philosophy instructs us to pay homage to the gods, not through hope or fear, but from veneration of their superior nature. It moreover enables us to conquer the fear of death, by teaching us that it is no proper object of terror; since, whilst we are, death is not, and when death arrives, we are not: so that it neither concerns the living nor the dead. The only evils to be apprehended are bodily pain, and distress of mind. Bodily pain it becomes a wise man to endure with patience and firmness; because, if it be slight, it may easily be borne; and if it be intense, it cannot last long. Mental distress commonly arises not from nature, but from opinion; a wise man will therefore arm himself against this kind of suffering, by reflecting that the gifts of fortune, the loss of which he may be inclined to deplore, were never his own, but depended upon circumstances which he could not command. If, therefore, they happen to leave him, he will endeavor, as soon as possible, to obliterate the remembrance of them, by occupying his mind in pleasant contemplation, and engaging in agreeable avocations.

"Justice respects man as living in society, and is the common bond without which no society can subsist. This virtue, like the rest, derives its value from its tendency to promote the happiness of life. Not only is it never injurious to the man who practices it, but nourishes-in his mind calm reflections and pleasant hopes; whereas it is impossible that the mind in which injustice dwells, should not be full of disquietude.—Since it is impossible that iniquitous actions should promote the enjoyment of life, as much as remorse of conscience, legal penalties, and public disgrace, must increase its troubles, every one who follows the dictates of sound reason, will practice the virtues of justice, equity, and fidelity. In society, the necessity of the mutual exercise of justice, in order to the common enjoyment of the gifts of nature, is the ground of those laws by which it is prescribed. It is the interest of every individual in a state to conform to the laws of justice; for by injuring no one, and rendering to every man his due, he contributes his part towards the preservation of that society, upon the perpetuity of which his own safety depends. Nor ought any one to think that he is at liberty to violate the rights of his fellow citizens, provided he can do it securely; for he who has committed an unjust action can never be certain that it will not be discovered; and however successfully he may conceal it from others, this will avail him little, since he cannot conceal it from himself. In different communities, different laws may be instituted, according to the circumstances of the people who compose them. Whatever is thus prescribed is to be considered as a rule of justice, so long as the society shall judge the observance of it to be for the benefit of the whole. But whenever any rule of conduct is found upon experience not to be conducive to the public good, being no longer useful, it should no longer be prescribed.

"Nearly allied to justice are the virtues of beneficence, compassion, gratitude, piety, and friendship.—He who confers benefits upon others, procures to himself the satisfaction of seeing the stream of plenty spreading around him from the fountain of his beneficence; at the same time, he enjoys the pleasure of being esteemed by others. The exercise of gratitude, filial affection, and reverence for the gods, is necessary, in order to avoid the hatred and contempt of all men. Friendships are contracted for the sake of mutual benefit; but by degrees they ripen into such disinterested attachment, that they are continued without any prospect of advantage. Between friends there is a kind of league, that each will love the other as himself. A true friend will partake of the wants and sorrows of his friend, as if they were his own; if he be in want, he will relieve him; if he be in prison, he will visit him; if he be sick, he will come to him; nay-situations may occur, in which he would not scruple to die for him. It cannot then be doubted, that friendship is one of the most useful means of procuring a secure, tranquil, and happy life."

No man will, we think, find anything in the foregoing summary to justify the foul language used against Epicurus, and his moral philosophy; the secret is in the physical doctrines, and this secret is, that Epicurus was actually, if not intentionally, an Atheist. The following is a summary of his physical doctrine:—

"Nothing can ever spring from nothing, nor can anything ever return to nothing. The universe always existed, and will always remain; for there is nothing into which it can be changed. There is nothing in Nature, nor can anything be conceived, besides body and space. Body is that which possesses the properties of bulk, figure, resistance, and gravity: it is this alone which can touch or be touched. Space is the region which is, or may be, occupied by body, and which affords it an opportunity of moving freely. That there are bodies in the universe is attested by the senses. That there is also space is evident; since otherwise bodies would have no place in which to move or exist, and of their existence and motion we have the certain proof of perception. Besides these, no third nature can be conceived; for such a nature must either have bulk and solidity, or want them; that is, it must either be body or space: this does not, however, preclude the existence of qualities, which have no subsistence but in the body to which they belong.

"The universe, consisting of body and space, is infinite, for it has no limits. Bodies are infinite in multitude; space is infinite in magnitude. The term above, or beneath, high or low, cannot be properly applied to infinite space. The universe is to be conceived as immoveable, since beyond it there is no place into which it can move; and as eternal and immutable, since it is neither liable to increase nor decrease, to production nor decay. Nevertheless, the parts of the universe are in motion, and are subject to change.

"All bodies consist of parts, of which they are composed, and into which they may be resolved; and these parts are either themselves simple principles, or may be resolved into such. These first principles, or simple atoms, are divisible by no force, and, therefore, must be immutable. This may also be inferred from the uniformity of Nature, which could not be preserved if its principles were not certain and consistent. The existence of such atoms is evident, since it is impossible that anything which exists should be reduced to nothing. A finite body cannot consist of parts infinite, either in magnitude or number; divisibility of bodies ad infinitum, is therefore conceivable. All atoms are of the same nature, or differ in no essential qualities—From their different effects upon the senses, it appears, however, that they differ in magnitude, figure, and weight. Atoms exist in every possible variety of figure—round, oval, conical, cubical, sharp, hooked, etc. But in every shape, they are, on account of their solidity, infrangible, or incapable of actual division.

"Gravity must be an essential property of atoms; for since they are perpetually in motion, or making an effort to move, they must be moved by an internal impulse, which may be called gravity.

"The principle of gravity, that internal energy which is the cause of all motion, whether simple or complex, being essential to the primary corpuscles or atoms, they must have been incessantly and from eternity in actual motion."

Epicurus, who boasts that he was an inquirer and a philosopher in his thirteenth year, was scarcely likely to bow his mind to the mythology of his country. The man who, when he was but a schoolboy, insisted upon an answer to the question, "Whence came chaos?" could hardly be expected to receive as admitted facts the fabulous legends as to Jupiter and the other gods. His theology is, however, in some respects, obscure, and unintelligible; for while he zealously opposed the popular fables, which men misname God-ideas, he at the same time admitted the existence of material gods, whom he placed in the intervals between the infinite worlds, where they passed a life undisturbed by aught, and enjoyed a happiness which does not admit of augmentation. These inactive gods play a strange part in the system of Epicurus; and it is asserted by many that these extraordinary conceptions of Deity were put forward by the philosopher to screen him from the consequences attaching to a charge of Atheism. Dr. Heinrich Ritter, who does not seem very friendly disposed towards Epicurus, or his philosophy, repudiates this notion, and argues Epicurus was not in truth an Atheist, and alleges that it was a mere pretence on his part; and that from his very theory of knowledge the existence of gods could be deduced. It is quite evident that Epicurus neither regarded "the gods" in the capacity of Creators, controllers, or rulers, so that his Theism (if it be Theism) twas not of a very superstitious character. The God who neither created man, nor exercised any influence whatever over his actions or thinkings, could have but little to do with man at all.

If we attempt to review the whole of the teachings of Epicurus, we and they are defective and imperfect in many respects, and necessarily so. We say necessarily so, because the imperfect science of the day limited the array of facts presented to the philosopher, and narrowed the base upon which he was to erect his system. We must expect, therefore, to find the structure weak in many points, because it was too large for the foundation; but we are not, therefore, to pass it on one side, and without further notice; it should rather be our task to lay good, wide, and sure foundations, on which to build up a system, and develop a method, really having, for its end, the happiness of mankind. We live 2000 years later than the Athenian philosopher.—In those 2000 years many facts have been dragged out of "the circle of the unknown and unused." Astronomy, geology, physiology, psychology—all except theology are belter understood. Men pretend they are searching after happiness, and where do they try to find it? Not here amongst the known, but in the possible hereafter amongst the unknowable. How do they try to find it? Not by the aid of the known, not by the light of facts, gathered in years of toil, and sanctified by the blood of some of the noblest of truth's noble martyrs; no—but in the darkness of the unknown and unknowable; in the next world. Question the men who fly to theology for happiness, and they will tell you that the most learned of the theologians sum up their knowledge in the word "incomprehensible." Is it wonderful that their happiness is somewhat marred "here" by quarrels as to the true definition of "hereafter?" G. H. Lewes says, of the Epicurean philosophy, "that the attempt failed because the basis was not broad enough. The Epicureans are therefore to be regarded as men who ventured on a great problem, and failed because they only saw part of the truth." And we might add that Christianity, and every other religious "anity," fails, because the professors expect to obtain happiness in the next life, and neglect to work for it in the present one.

Epicurus says, no life can be pleasant except a virtuous life; and he charges you to avoid whatever maybe calculated to create disquiet in the mind, or give pain to the body. The Rev. Habbakuk Smilenot, of little Bethel, says that all pleasure here, is vanity and vexation in the hereafter; and he charges you to continually worry and harass your mind with fears that you may be condemned to hell, and doubts whether you will be permitted to enter heaven. Which is the best, the philosophy of Epicurus, or the theology of Smilenot?

G. H. Lewes says:—"Epicureanism, in leading man to a correct appreciation of the moral end of his existence, in showing him how to be truly happy, has to combat with many obstructions which hide from him the real road of life. These obstructions are his illusions, his prejudices, his errors, his ignorance. This ignorance is of two kinds, as Victor Cousin points out; ignorance of the laws of the external world, which creates absurd superstitions, and troubles the mind with false fears and false hopes. Hence the necessity of some knowledge of physics." (We can scarcely blame Epicurus that he was not in advance of his time, as far as the physical sciences are concerned, and therefore imparted an imperfect system of physics. We must, with our improved knowledge, ourselves remove the obstruction.) "The second kind of ignorance is that of the nature of man. Socrates had taught men to regard their own nature as the great object of investigation; and this lesson Epicurus willingly gave ear to.—But man does not interrogate his own nature out of simple curiosity, or simple erudition; he studies his nature in order that he may improve it; he learns the extent of his capacities, in order that he may properly direct them. The aim, therefore, of all such inquiries must be happiness."

We may add that the result of all such inquiries will be happiness, if the inquirer will but base his investigation and experiments upon facts. Let him understand that, as he improves the circumstances which surround him, so will he advance himself, becoming happier, and making his fellows happy also. Remember the words of Epicurus, and seek that pleasure for yourself which appears the most durable, and attended with the greatest pleasure to your fellow men.

"I"

CPSIA information can be obtained
at www.ICGtesting.com
Printed in the USA
LVHW011511241219
641607LV00005B/753

9 781523 790074